RZIM Critical Questions Discussion Guides

What Is Truth?

Paul Copan & Mark Linville

SERIES EDITOR Ravi Zacharias

GENERAL EDITOR Danielle DuRant

Inter-Varsity Press
Nottingham, England

IVP Connect
An imprint of InterVarsity Press
Downers Grove, Illinois

InterVarsity Press
P.O. Box 1400, Downers Grove, IL 60515-1426
World Wide Web: www.ivpress.com
Email: email@ivpress.com

Inter-Varsity Press, England
Norton Street, Nottingham NG7 3HR, England
Website: www.ivpbooks.com
Email: ivp@ivpbooks.com

©2007 by Ravi Zacharias International Ministries

All rights reserved. No part of this book may be reproduced, stored in a retrieval system or transmitted in any form or by any means, electronic, mechanical, photocopying, recording or otherwise, without the prior permission of InterVarsity Press.

Published in association with the literary agency of Wolgemuth & Associates, Inc., Orlando, Florida.

InterVarsity Press®️ is the book-publishing division of InterVarsity Christian Fellowship/USA®️, a student movement active on campus at hundreds of universities, colleges and schools of nursing in the United States of America, and a member movement of the International Fellowship of Evangelical Students. For information about local and regional activities, write Public Relations Dept., InterVarsity Christian Fellowship/USA, 6400 Schroeder Rd., P.O. Box 7895, Madison, WI 53707-7895, or visit the IVCF website at <www.intervarsity.org>.

Inter-Varsity Press, England, is closely linked with the Universities and Colleges Christian Fellowship, a student movement connecting Christian Unions in universities and colleges throughout Great Britain, and a member movement of the International Fellowship of Evangelical Students. Website: www.uccf.org.uk.

All Scripture quotations, unless otherwise indicated, are taken from the Holy Bible, New International Version®️. NIV®️. *Copyright ©1973, 1978, 1984 by International Bible Society. Used by permission of Zondervan Publishing House. All rights reserved.*

Adapted from Paul Copan, Is Everything Really Relative? *(Norcross, Ga.: RZIM, 1999) and Mark Linville,* Is Everything Permitted? *(Norcross, Ga.: RZIM, 2001).*

Design: Cindy Kiple
Images: David Buffington/Getty Images

USA ISBN 978-0-8308-3154-8
UK ISBN 978-1-84474-223-3

Printed in the United States of America ∞

| P | 19 | 18 | 17 | 16 | 15 | 14 | 13 | 12 | 11 | 10 | 9 | 8 | 7 | 6 | 5 | 4 | 3 | 2 | 1 |
| Y | 23 | 22 | 21 | 20 | 19 | 18 | 17 | 16 | 15 | 14 | 13 | 12 | 11 | 10 | 09 | 08 | 07 | | | |

Contents

Introduction

I was at an airport looking for my departure gate, and I noticed that the flight listed was to another city. So I asked a passenger if that flight was headed to Atlanta or elsewhere. She promptly answered my question and told me the notation was wrong. As I thanked her and turned to find a seat, she said, "Are you Ravi Zacharias?" I answered yes. Then came this utterly surprising response: "I listen to you on the radio regularly. I didn't know you had questions as well." I laughed at her compliment and assured her that I had several questions, especially if I want to get to the right destination.

There are so many answers out there and a question to every answer. To ask them is to engage with information. To ask questions about life's ultimate questions is to be in the pursuit of God. That's what this series is about: to take you to the heart and mind of God, which is the right destination.

In this series, critical questions raised by thinking minds are answered by those who have asked them themselves, and found the answer in the person and teaching of Jesus Christ. There are writers in this series that I have heavily leaned on myself. They are trained in the art of critical thinking not merely for the intellectual stimulation it brings but for the ultimate pursuit: the bridge between the heart and the mind so that thinking shapes being, which in turn impels doing.

In our time such helps as this series are invaluable. On every side, be it the academy or the movies, just enough doubt is cast on the person of Jesus that minds are left unsteadied in their trust in the Scriptures and the truth claims of the gospel. Such doubts and questionings are rarely answered by a one-blow argument. Life is not as simple as that. In fact, any worldview that depends on one such knockout argument flirts with logical and experiential extinction.

Life closes in on us from multiple sides. That is why a good apologetic starts with the fundamentals before it deals with the specifics. From the nature of truth to the incarnation of it in Jesus, from the trustworthiness of the Scriptures to the questions of moral reasoning, they are addressed here. These succinct and interactive discussion guides will stir your mind and occupy a much-used section in your library.

I sincerely hope this series will be both a tool of equipment and a source of inspiration. Darrell Bock in his study *Can I Trust the Bible?* sums up the content of these slender volumes well:

> If there is the possibility that God has spoken through this text and has participated in the history it records, then the answers to our questions are not a mere academic exercise. Our journey back into these seemingly foreign, ancient times may be a real opportunity to see more clearly who we are and were created to be.

A couple words of appreciation are well in order. First, the original effort in putting this all together was done by Paul Copan. In this instance, the hard work as general editor is by Danielle DuRant, who labored long to make this accessible. I am also grateful to InterVarsity Press for seeing the value in this short series and taking the step to publish it. Those of us who study this material will be the beneficiaries.

Questions will haunt as long as the mind is alive. The answers of Christ will inspire and instruct because he is the author of life.

Ravi Zacharias

"Objective truth is unavoidable," observes Paul Copan in his booklet *Is Everything Really Relative?* (Norcross, Ga.: RZIM, 1999). "After all, if we attempt to reject it, we'll do so on the basis of reasons we take to be true, and not false. But if objective truth, reality, and morality exist, then this has certain implications for me. It means living in accordance with these truths rather than pretending they don't exist" (p. 49). Indeed, adds Mark Linville, "The very notion of human dignity makes sense only if God exists" (*Is Everything Permissible?* [Norcross, Ga.: RZIM, 2001], p. 54).

In this discussion guide we will examine various reasons why truth is objective and relativism is ultimately unlivable. Though our culture esteems tolerance, we will explore its limits and the question whether judgments are inevitable. Lastly, we will consider how objective moral values must necessarily come from God—a God who reveals himself to be good and worthy of our worship.

■ SUGGESTIONS FOR INDIVIDUAL STUDY

1. As you begin each session, pray that God will speak to you through his Word.

2. Read the introduction to the session and respond to the opening reflection question or exercise. This is designed to help you focus on God and on the theme of the session.

3. Each session considers a particular passage or passages of Scripture, and is supplemented by the author's commentary. Read and reread the text before engaging the questions.

4. Write your answers to the questions in the spaces provided or in a personal journal. Writing can bring clarity and deeper understanding of yourself and of God's Word.

5. It might be good to have a Bible dictionary handy. Use it to look up any unfamiliar words, names or places.

■ SUGGESTIONS FOR MEMBERS OF A GROUP STUDY

1. Come to the study prepared. Follow the suggestions for individual study mentioned above. You will find that careful preparation will greatly enrich your time spent in group discussion.

2. Be willing to participate in the discussion. The leader of your group will not be lecturing. Instead, he or she will be encouraging the members of the group to discuss what they have learned. The leader will be asking the questions that are found in this guide.

3. Stick to the topic being discussed. Your answers should be based on the texts provided and not on outside authorities such as commentaries or speakers. Only rarely should you refer to other portions of the Bible. This allows for everyone to participate in in-depth study on equal ground.

4. Be sensitive to the other members of the group. Listen attentively when they describe what they have learned. You may be surprised by their insights! Each question assumes a variety of answers. Many questions do not have "right" answers, particularly questions that aim at meaning or application. Instead the questions push us to explore the topic more thoroughly. When possible, link what you say to the comments of others. Also, be affirming whenever you can. This will encourage some of the more hesitant members of the group to participate.

5. Be careful not to dominate the discussion. We are sometimes so eager to express our thoughts that we leave too little opportunity for others to respond. By all means participate! But allow others to also.

6. Expect God to teach you through the material being discussed and through the other members of the group. Pray that you will have an enjoyable and profitable time together, but also that as a result of the study you will find ways that you can take action individually and/or as a group.

7. Remember that anything said in the group is considered confidential and should not be discussed outside the group unless specific permission is given to do so.

8. If you are the group leader, you will find additional suggestions at the back of the guide.

1 Does Relativism Work?

What is true must correspond to reality; otherwise, it is false. Therefore if *truth* means anything at all, *it must exclude something*—namely, *falsehood*.

■ OPEN

When did you first learn that Santa Claus and the Easter Bunny weren't real? How did you respond to the news?

■ STUDY

The book of Joshua records Israel's entry into and sojourn in the Promised Land, after many years of bondage in Egypt and wandering without a home. As his days on earth are waning, Joshua assembles the people to renew the covenant God established with them through Moses at Mount Sinai. The prophet reminds his audience of God's long faithfulness to them. In this section of the covenant, the LORD God sets an explicit choice before his people: You must choose whom you will serve. **Read Joshua 24:14-28.**

¹⁴*"Now fear the LORD and serve him with all faithfulness. Throw away the gods your forefathers worshiped beyond the River and in*

Egypt, and serve the LORD. ^{15}But if serving the LORD seems undesirable to you, then choose for yourselves this day whom you will serve, whether the gods your forefathers served beyond the River, or the gods of the Amorites, in whose land you are living. But as for me and my household, we will serve the LORD."

^{16}Then the people answered, "Far be it from us to forsake the LORD to serve other gods! ^{17}It was the LORD our God himself who brought us and our fathers up out of Egypt, from that land of slavery, and performed those great signs before our eyes. He protected us on our entire journey and among all the nations through which we traveled. ^{18}And the LORD drove out before us all the nations, including the Amorites, who lived in the land. We too will serve the LORD, because he is our God."

^{19}Joshua said to the people, "You are not able to serve the LORD. He is a holy God; he is a jealous God. He will not forgive your rebellion and your sins. ^{20}If you forsake the LORD and serve foreign gods, he will turn and bring disaster on you and make an end of you, after he has been good to you."

^{21}But the people said to Joshua, "No! We will serve the LORD."

^{22}Then Joshua said, "You are witnesses against yourselves that you have chosen to serve the LORD."

"Yes, we are witnesses," they replied.

^{23}"Now then," said Joshua, "throw away the foreign gods that are among you and yield your hearts to the LORD, the God of Israel."

^{24}And the people said to Joshua, "We will serve the LORD our God and obey him."

^{25}On that day Joshua made a covenant for the people, and there at Shechem he drew up for them decrees and laws. ^{26}And Joshua recorded these things in the Book of the Law of God. Then he took a large stone and set it up there under the oak near the holy place of the LORD.

^{27}"See!" he said to all the people. "This stone will be a witness *against us. It has heard all the words the* LORD *has said to us. It will be a witness against you if you are untrue to your God."*

²⁸*Then Joshua sent the people away, each to his own inheritance.*

1. Note the number of times the verb *serve* appears in this passage. Why do you think this word is repeated so often? What emotions does it elicit for you?

2. What choice is offered in verse 15?

How does it affirm the character of God and his covenant?

3. What do you make of Joshua's response in verse 19: "You are not able to serve the LORD"? If you were standing before Joshua, how might you respond to his charge?

4. "Jealous" is usually understood negatively, yet in the context of an exclusive relationship such as marriage it is important to be jealous of certain boundaries and commitments. How does this example apply to verses 19 and 20?

A 1994 poll by the Barna Group revealed that 72 percent of American adults—that's almost three out of four—agreed with the statement that there is "no such thing as absolute truth; two people could define truth in totally conflicting ways, but both still be correct."

That's what *relativism* is: A belief can be true for one person but not for another. "If you believe that Christianity is right for you, that's fine. I'm glad it works for you. I just happen to believe differently. But I'm not going to say that you're wrong," the relativist will declare.

We can ask the relativist: "Do you believe that relativism is true? If it's true, is it *absolutely* true for everyone, or is it just true for you?" Now if the relativist says that his view is true for *everyone*, then it is no longer relative but absolute. Thus the view is self-contradictory and therefore false.

But what if the relativist says, "This is just my view; it's just true for me, and you don't have to believe it"? Well, if *this* is the relativist's position, then what he is saying is on the same level of asserting, "Vanilla ice cream tastes better to you, but chocolate tastes better to me." So the relativist is saying *nothing* that is worthy of being believed by another; he is just giving his own opinion. But usually relativists believe they are giving more than their own opinion. In fact, the famous relativistic slogan—"That's true for *you*, but not for me"—presupposes that relativism applies to at least *two people*! The relativist believes that relativism is true for *both* parties, not just one.

5. Define relativism in your own words.

6. In what ways is relativism self-contradictory?

> The logical system is built on four fundamental laws, laws that are impossible to argue against without at the same time proving them. For the sake of brevity, let me discuss just two of them.
>
> First is the Law of Noncontradiction. This law affirms that no two contradictory statements can be both true and false at the same time in the same sense. To deny the Law of Noncontradiction is only to affirm it, for to say that the Law of Noncontradiction is not true is to assume that the denial is true and the law is not. But that is precisely what the law says—that two contradictory statements cannot both be true. There is no way to get around this.
>
> The second foundational law is the Law of Rational Inference. By that we mean that inferences can be made from what is known to what is unknown. No one could prove any point without the Law of Rational Inference. There are conclusions that may be legitimately drawn when statements are true and the argument containing those statements is valid. . . .
>
> In short, therefore, truth boils down to two tests: Statements must correspond to reality, and any system of thought that is developed as a result must be coherent. The correspondence and coherence tests are applied by all of us in matters that affect us.

> Therefore, when Jesus said, "I am the way and the truth and the life. No man comes to the father except through me," He was making a very reasonable statement by affirming truth's exclusivity. The question one may legitimately ask is whether He demonstrated that claim rather than just stating it.[1]

7. How does the Law of Noncontradiction reveal the inconsistency of relativism?

8. In what ways has relativism misinformed our understanding of religious belief?

9. What does it mean to say that truth is, by definition, exclusive?

---

[1]Ravi Zacharias, *Deliver Us from Evil: Resorting the Soul in a Disintegrating Culture* (Dallas: Word, 1996), pp. 220-21.

10. Look again at verses 14-15 and 19-20. How does the idea that truth necessarily excludes help us to comprehend the character of God depicted in these verses?

11. How might an understanding of the inconsistency of relativism and the inescapability of absolute truth assist you today in your own spiritual journey?

■ GOING FURTHER

Spend some time thinking and perhaps journaling about your response to question 11. Make a note of questions that you may want to revisit or talk to someone about after completing this booklet.

Additional Reading

For one of the best discussions on the question of relativism and absolute truth, see the first section of C. S. Lewis's classic book *Mere Christianity,* "Right and Wrong as a Clue to the Meaning in the Universe."

2 | Is Sincerity Enough?

ACTS 26:1-29

Reality is objective. This means that no matter how much we think we shape reality, at some point we must admit that some of our very own beliefs (like the assumption that we can create any reality we want) are themselves *immune* to human manipulation. Simply by sincerely believing won't change the fact that my favorite baseball team, the Cleveland Indians, lost the World Series to the Atlanta Braves in 1995 and then to the Florida Marlins in 1997.

■ OPEN

Recall some childhood experiences of playing "make-believe." Who were the characters? What places did you visit or victories did you win?

■ STUDY

In the book of Acts, Luke records the early church's rapid growth from Jerusalem to Rome after Jesus' resurrection and ascension. Along with this growth came persecution. At the stoning of Stephen we are introduced to Saul, who later becomes Jesus' apostle Paul and suffers intense hardship. Shuffled between imprisonment in Jerusalem and trials before two Roman governors,

Paul is finally brought to stand before King Agrippa. **Read Acts 26:1-29.**

¹*Then Agrippa said to Paul, "You have permission to speak for yourself."*

So Paul motioned with his hand and began his defense: ²*"King Agrippa, I consider myself fortunate to stand before you today as I make my defense against all the accusations of the Jews,* ³*and especially so because you are well acquainted with all the Jewish customs and controversies. Therefore, I beg you to listen to me patiently.*

⁴*The Jews all know the way I have lived ever since I was a child, from the beginning of my life in my own country, and also in Jerusalem.* ⁵*They have known me for a long time and can testify, if they are willing, that according to the strictest sect of our religion, I lived as a Pharisee.* ⁶*And now it is because of my hope in what God has promised our fathers that I am on trial today.* ⁷*This is the promise our twelve tribes are hoping to see fulfilled as they earnestly serve God day and night. O king, it is because of this hope that the Jews are accusing me.* ⁸*Why should any of you consider it incredible that God raises the dead?*

⁹*I too was convinced that I ought to do all that was possible to oppose the name of Jesus of Nazareth.* ¹⁰*And that is just what I did in Jerusalem. On the authority of the chief priests I put many of the saints in prison, and when they were put to death, I cast my vote against them.* ¹¹*Many a time I went from one synagogue to another to have them punished, and I tried to force them to blaspheme. In my obsession against them, I even went to foreign cities to persecute them.*

¹²*On one of these journeys I was going to Damascus with the authority and commission of the chief priests.* ¹³*About noon, O king, as I was on the road, I saw a light from heaven, brighter than the sun,*

blazing around me and my companions. ¹⁴We all fell to the ground, and I heard a voice saying to me in Aramaic, 'Saul, Saul, why do you persecute me? It is hard for you to kick against the goads.'"

¹⁵"Then I asked, 'Who are you, Lord?'

" 'I am Jesus, whom you are persecuting,' the Lord replied. ¹⁶'Now get up and stand on your feet. I have appeared to you to appoint you as a servant and as a witness of what you have seen of me and what I will show you. ¹⁷I will rescue you from your own people and from the Gentiles. I am sending you to them ¹⁸to open their eyes and turn them from darkness to light, and from the power of Satan to God, so that they may receive forgiveness of sins and a place among those who are sanctified by faith in me.'

¹⁹"So then, King Agrippa, I was not disobedient to the vision from heaven. ²⁰First to those in Damascus, then to those in Jerusalem and in all Judea, and to the Gentiles also, I preached that they should repent and turn to God and prove their repentance by their deeds. ²¹That is why the Jews seized me in the temple courts and tried to kill me. ²²But I have had God's help to this very day, and so I stand here and testify to small and great alike. I am saying nothing beyond what the prophets and Moses said would happen— ²³that the Christ would suffer and, as the first to rise from the dead, would proclaim light to his own people and to the Gentiles."

²⁴At this point Festus interrupted Paul's defense. "You are out of your mind, Paul!" he shouted. "Your great learning is driving you insane."

²⁵"I am not insane, most excellent Festus," Paul replied. "What I am saying is true and reasonable. ²⁶The king is familiar with these things, and I can speak freely to him. I am convinced that none of this has escaped his notice, because it was not done in a corner. ²⁷King Agrippa, do you believe the prophets? I know you do."

[28]*Then Agrippa said to Paul, "Do you think that in such a short time you can persuade me to be a Christian?"*

[29]*Paul replied, "Short time or long—I pray God that not only you but all who are listening to me today may become what I am, except for these chains."*

1. What information do we gather about both King Agrippa's and Paul's character in verses 2-5?

2. Why is Paul on trial (see verses 6-7)?

3. How does the apostle present the precise charge against him in verse 8? Why do you think he does this?

4. What proof does Paul offer of his sincere commitment to his religious faith and position as a Pharisee (see verses 9-11)?

One commonly held belief is "Truth is what you sincerely be-lieve." Sincerity, according to this statement, makes some-thing true—a kind of reality-creation. But I can think of a lot of things that are false or wrong no matter how sincerely one might believe that they are "true" or "good"—sincere serial-killing, sincere rape, sincere torture, sincere random shoot-ings, sincere Fascism, sincere Satanism. Sincerity does not make 2+2=5, nor does it alter the law of gravity. Simply by sincerely believing, I can't bring my lost loved one back from the dead.

Furthermore, this "sincere-belief" criterion for truth says, in essence, "You are *wrong* and *mistaken* if you disagree with my view that sincere belief makes something true." So the person who believes that reality is *not* created by sincerity can reply: "What if I *sincerely believe* that that believing something sincerely *does not* make something true?"

5. Explain why sincerely believing something is an inadequate test of whether it is true or not.

6. What is self-contradictory in the idea that sincere belief dic-tates what is true?

You hear it a thousand times and more growing up in the East—"We all come through different routes and end up in the same place." But I say to you, God is not a place or an ex-perience or a feeling. Pluralistic cultures are beguiled by the cosmetically courteous idea that sincerity or privilege of birth is all that counts and that truth is subject to the beholder. In no other discipline of life can one be so naive as to claim inherited belief or insistent belief as the sole determiner of truth. Why, then, do we make the catastrophic error of thinking that all religions are right and that it does not matter whether the claims they make are objectively true?

All religions are not the same. All religions do not point to God. All religions *do not say* that all religions are the same. At the heart of *every* religion is an uncompromising commitment to a particular way of defining who God is or is not and accordingly, of defining life's purpose. Anyone who claims that all religions are the same betrays not only an ignorance of all religions but a caricatured view of even the best-known ones. Every religion at its core is exclusive.[2]

7. Why, do you think, do people "make the catastrophic error of thinking that all religions are right and that it does not matter whether the claims they make are objectively true"?

8. Look again at Acts 26. What does it mean "to kick against the goads" (see verse 14)? How does this proverb contribute to the understanding that reality is objective?

---

[2]Ravi Zacharias, *Jesus Among Other Gods* (Nashville: Word Publishing, 2000), pp. 6-7.

9. What does Jesus tell Paul to do, and what is his response?

How do you think Paul felt when he learned that he had misjudged Jesus?

10. Why do you think Festus interrupts Paul?

11. What do we learn from Paul about Agrippa's beliefs?

What do you think keeps Agrippa from becoming what Paul has become?

■ GOING FURTHER

Consider journaling and perhaps talking further to someone about your own experience of changing beliefs. What factors contributed to your change in understanding? Was it difficult to let go of certain ideas? Why?

Additional Reading

For a more extensive discussion on the nature of truth and other worldviews, see pages 121-31 of Ravi Zacharias's book *Can Man Live Without God?* (Dallas: Word, 1994).

3 | Are Judgments Inevitable?

1 CORINTHIANS 5

Relativism has its ironies. Despite the fact that it proclaims a freedom from absolute truth, relativists still hold to the absolute of tolerance. If there is *anything* that is morally wrong today, it is intolerance! Again, we have another contradiction within relativism—besides the *absolute denial* of absolutes, we have the *absolute wrongness* of intolerance!

■ OPEN

What are some of your pet peeves? How do they affect your interactions with other people?

■ STUDY

The apostle Paul writes to the church in Corinth upon hearing reports of serious division and immorality. He describes what true judgment looks like: recognizing that God is the ultimate judge, it seeks to restore the offender to right relationship with God and others. Paul is forthright and passionate, longing that this dysfunctional fellowship feast on "the bread of sincerity and truth" (verse 8). *Read 1 Corinthians 5.*

¹*It is actually reported that there is sexual immorality among you,*

and of a kind that does not occur even among pagans: A man has his father's wife. ²And you are proud! Shouldn't you rather have been filled with grief and have put out of your fellowship the man who did this? ³Even though I am not physically present, I am with you in spirit. And I have already passed judgment on the one who did this, just as if I were present. ⁴When you are assembled in the name of our Lord Jesus and I am with you in spirit, and the power of our Lord Jesus is present, ⁵hand this man over to Satan, so that the sinful nature may be destroyed and his spirit saved on the day of the Lord.

⁶Your boasting is not good. Don't you know that a little yeast works through the whole batch of dough? ⁷Get rid of the old yeast that you may be a new batch without yeast—as you really are. For Christ, our Passover lamb, has been sacrificed. ⁸Therefore let us keep the Festival, not with the old yeast, the yeast of malice and wickedness, but with bread without yeast, the bread of sincerity and truth.

⁹I have written you in my letter not to associate with sexually immoral people— ¹⁰not at all meaning the people of this world who are immoral, or the greedy and swindlers, or idolaters. In that case you would have to leave this world. ¹¹But now I am writing you that you must not associate with anyone who calls himself a brother but is sexually immoral or greedy, an idolater or a slanderer, a drunkard or a swindler. With such a man do not even eat.

¹²What business is it of mine to judge those outside the church? Are you not to judge those inside? ¹³God will judge those outside. "Expel the wicked man from among you."

1. What are your initial reactions to what Paul describes in verses 1 and 2?

2. Why do you think this church would be proud of the reports Paul has received about it?

3. Who does Paul pass judgment on, and what does he urge the church to do (verses 3-5)?

Does his language startle or offend you? Why or why not?

> A lot of people think that if you believe you are right and someone else is wrong, then you are being intolerant. But this is a misunderstanding. Historically, tolerance has been defined as "putting up with beliefs one takes to be erroneous or false." In fact, we often use *tolerance* in this way today. Most people tolerate Brussels sprouts or liver when served it as guests, but no one tolerates what he enjoys (chocolate or ice cream). Today, though, some people have said that tolerance means "*accepting* all views as true and not saying any are false." But if we define tolerance this way, then we'll start accepting views that contradict one another. The relativist will be put in the awkward spot of believing *his* view—that everything is relative—and *my* view—that *absolutes* exist. But the relativist *by definition* cannot accept an absolutist's view as true.

4. How has the definition of *tolerance* changed over time?

5. Paul illustrates the effects on a body when contradictory views are tolerated and even celebrated (verses 6-7). Explain.

6. What is the contrast depicted in verse 8?

7. Do you ever catch yourself trying to reconcile two opposing views? How do you avoid rationalizing or dismissing beliefs in the process?

Tolerance, *properly* understood, means that we respect people enough to permit them to hold their beliefs even if we profoundly disagree with them. Tolerance says that *all people should be accepted as possessing dignity and thus as being worthy of respect.* This does not mean we have to accept their views as true or that they are worthy of belief. True tolerance distinguishes between *people* and *beliefs;* genuine tolerance is the acceptance and respectful treatment of other people— *even if* we don't accept their views. Remember that the relativist will *never* accept the absolutist's view as true or legitimate. And you've probably noticed how some people can say that we should accept all views as true—*until* they talk to someone who doesn't accept all views as true! At this point, all logic often stops, and insulting begins!

8. What does true tolerance look like?

9. Are there some things that should never be tolerated? Why?

10. The apostle Paul is careful to communicate that we all deserve judgment and that God alone is judge (see verses 9-13). How might this perspective help you this week?

■ GOING FURTHER

Look again at question 7. Can you think of a specific instance or habit in which you attempt to reconcile two opposing views? (For example, the impulse to relax versus the need to work or study.) Take time to write further about your response. As you feel comfortable, consider talking to someone about it.

Additional Reading

For a broader examination of tolerance in relation to Christianity, see Amy Orr-Ewing's *Is the Bible Intolerant?* (Downers Grove, Ill.: InterVarsity Press, 2006).

4 | Can We Have Moral Values Without God?

People will say they don't care about sexual morality or cheating on exams. But they become moral absolutists in a hurry when someone steals *their* things or violates *their* rights. That is, they are *selective* moral relativists. It's okay for anyone to do anything—*until* it disrupts *my* life or violates *my* rights. *Then* it's time to become a moral absolutist!

■ OPEN

When someone cuts you off in traffic, how do you react? How is your mood affected? What about when you cut someone off in traffic?

■ STUDY

The book of Romans unfolds God's story of salvation. Its opening chapters affirm that each of us perceives God's voice through the splendor of his creation and through our conscience—the moral law written on our hearts. Though we may deny God's existence, we cannot deny the reality of a fixed moral law, and we prove it when we judge others by a standard that we ourselves break. *Read Romans 1:16-20, 28-32; 2:1-4.*

¹·¹⁶*I am not ashamed of the gospel, because it is the power of God for the salvation of everyone who believes: first for the Jew, then for the Gentile.* ¹⁷*For in the gospel a righteousness from God is revealed, a righteousness that is by faith from first to last, just as it is written: "The righteous will live by faith."*

¹⁸*The wrath of God is being revealed from heaven against all the godlessness and wickedness of men who suppress the truth by their wickedness,* ¹⁹*since what may be known about God is plain to them, because God has made it plain to them.* ²⁰*For since the creation of the world God's invisible qualities—his eternal power and divine nature—have been clearly seen, being understood from what has been made, so that men are without excuse. . . .*

²⁸*Furthermore, since they did not think it worthwhile to retain the knowledge of God, he gave them over to a depraved mind, to do what ought not to be done.* ²⁹*They have become filled with every kind of wickedness, evil, greed and depravity. They are full of envy, murder, strife, deceit and malice. They are gossips,* ³⁰*slanderers, God-haters, insolent, arrogant and boastful; they invent ways of doing evil; they disobey their parents;* ³¹*they are senseless, faithless, heartless, ruthless.* ³²*Although they know God's righteous decree that those who do such things deserve death, they not only continue to do these very things but also approve of those who practice them.*

²·¹*You, therefore, have no excuse, you who pass judgment on someone else, for at whatever point you judge the other, you are condemning yourself, because you who pass judgment do the same things.* ²*Now we know that God's judgment against those who do such things is based on truth.* ³*So when you a mere man, pass judgment on them and yet do the same things, do you think you will escape God's judgment?* ⁴*Or do you show contempt for the riches of his kindness, tolerance and patience, not realizing that God's kindness leads you toward repentance?*

1. Consider the three qualities associated with the gospel (see verses 16-17). What do these words communicate to you?

2. According to verse 18, what are we prone to do with the truth? Why do you think this is so?

3. We encounter a forthright description of human beings' position toward God in verses 18-20. What does it mean that we are "without excuse"?

4. Have you ever heard the expression "You become what you worship?" How have you found this proverb to be true in your own life, whether positively or negatively?

How does this proverb apply to Paul's words in verses 28-32?

When we are willing to ask *serious* questions about morality, we find that we don't *really* believe that moral values are
relative. Just ask yourself: "Do you *right now* believe that it's
okay to murder or to be murdered?" You might think: "Well,
some people have thought so." But the question is: "Do
you—not other people—*right now* have any doubt about the
wrongness of murder?" *This* is the place to begin—not what
other people have alleged. So we don't have to waste our time
talking about what we both accept as true. We can, instead,
begin discussing the real issue—namely, which viewpoint
best accounts for the existence of objective moral values.

But not only is moral relativism rationally problematic. It
is also *practically unlivable.* That is, we human beings—even
if we are *blind* to certain moral defects within us or our culture, can *still recognize* the violation of certain human rights
and basic moral standards when they confront us.

5. What is it about moral relativism—the notion that there is no
such thing as an absolute moral standard—that makes it intuitively implausible?

6. What about moral relativism makes it practically unlivable?

The Christian philosopher J. P. Moreland was speaking in a
dorm, and a relativistic student who lived there told him, "If
something works for you because you believe it, that's great.
But no one should force his or her views on other people
since everything is relative." J. P. told him that his view implied that there was no such thing as sin or wrongdoing, and

> the student readily agreed. Then as J. P. left, he unplugged
> the student's stereo and started out the door with it.
>   The student protested: "Hey, what are you doing? You can't
> do that!"
>   J. P. replied, "You're not going to *force* on me the belief that
> it is wrong to steal your stereo, are you?"

7. How does the relativist's position undercut the reality of sin or wrongdoing?

8. According to the student's view, did J. P. Moreland have the right to walk away with his stereo? Why?

9. Look at Romans 2:1. How does this verse provide further insight into this incident?

10. What qualities characterize God's judgment (see Romans 2:2, 4)?

What might your relationships look like if you emulated these same qualities?

11. Read again Romans 1:16-18. How might we be empowered to live right before God and others?

Does this idea make sense to you? Why or why not?

■ GOING FURTHER

Take time to read Romans 3:21-26 and Romans 5 and 6, where Paul explains the righteousness that comes from God. Write out your thoughts and questions about these chapters, especially in relation to this study.

Additional Reading

C. S. Lewis scholar Art Lindsley examines the way Lewis dealt with the question of moral relativism in his book *C. S. Lewis's Case for Christ: Insights from Reason, Imagination and Faith* (Downers Grove, Ill.: InterVarsity Press, 2005). See chapter 11, "Relativism: Aren't Morals Relative?"

5 | Why Should We Be Good?

LUKE 6:27–36

In his book *The Real Face of Atheism,* Ravi Zacharias notes that "religion that is based on truth, when reduced merely to a sociological function, will disintegrate through abuse. Time has proven, in an even stronger voice, that pragmatism, which by definition is to do whatever works, in the long run does not work because it is captive to the moment. The foundation of moral action must go deeper and farther than utilitarianism."

■ OPEN

Recall a time when you were a child and did something wrong without your parents or authority figures ever having a clue. How did "getting away with it" affect your behavior? What ultimately caused you to stop doing it?

■ STUDY

Jesus' teaching is both inspiring and difficult, as evidenced in his Sermon on the Plain, a shorter version of his Sermon on the Mount. Luke tells us that after he "spent the night praying to God" (Luke 6:12), Jesus calls his twelve disciples and then addresses a larger group that "has come to hear him and to be healed of their diseases" (verse 18). New Testament scholar Darrell Bock suggests that Jesus' sermon here is "the Gospel equivalent of Paul's chapter on love, 1 Corinthians 13." Moreover, verse 31 is recognized as one of the most significant ideas not only in all of Scripture but in moral philosophy as well. **Read Luke 6:27-36.**

27"But I tell you who hear me: Love your enemies, do good to those who hate you, 28bless those who curse you, pray for those who mistreat you. 29If someone strikes you on one cheek, turn to him the other also. If someone takes your cloak, do not stop him from taking your tunic. 30Give to everyone who asks you, and if anyone takes what belongs to you, do not demand it back. 31Do to others as you would have them do to you.

32"If you love those who love you, what credit is that to you? Even 'sinners' love those who love them. 33And if you do good to those who are good to you, what credit is that to you? Even 'sinners' do that. 34And if you lend to those from whom you expect repayment, what credit is that to you? Even 'sinners' lend to 'sinners,' expecting to be repaid in full. 35But love your enemies, do good to them, and lend to them without expecting to get anything back. Then your reward will be great, and you will be sons of the Most High, because he is kind to the ungrateful and wicked. 36Be merciful, just as your Father is merciful."

1. What is your initial reaction to Jesus' instruction in the first part of verse 27?

If you had the opportunity to interject or ask him a question at this point, what might you say?

2. How do Jesus' next three commands in verses 27-28 offer insight about his first one?

What does this insight tell us about his view of love?

3. Jesus' proclamation in verse 31 is recognized as perhaps the most important moral injunction in the history of philosophy and religion. Why do you think it is universally affirmed?

Utilitarians maintain that the difference between right and wrong actions is determined by their *consequences*, good or bad, for the "moral community."

Historically, mainstream utilitarianism has affirmed that *pleasure* is the one thing that is good or valuable for its own sake. Anything that may justly be labeled "good" is either pleasurable itself, or it directly or indirectly produces pleasure. To say that an action has good consequences will then be to say that it produces pleasure.

Even at its best, any utilitarian theory worthy of the name will insist that all moral duties are duties to promote *social utility.* Thus, if it is wrong for me to lie to you, the wrongness of such an action is found in the fact that it is, ultimately, bad *for society* at large. The wrongness of rape is not explained simply by saying that the *victim* is wronged. The would-be rapist has, at best, an indirect duty *regarding* the victim, and this indirect duty is derived from his *direct* duty to maintain the greatest possible net utility for the community. Here I am inclined to say, "Right answer; wrong reasons."

4. How does a utilitarian (or pragmatist or hedonist) decide what is good?

5. What concerns you about making ethical decisions based on the greatest good of the many as opposed to the one?

If God existed, we would certainly *expect* objective moral values to exist. Such values would not be surprising or unnatural at all. After all, if we humans have been made to resemble God in certain important respects, if we have been created in the "image" of a personal, good God (as traditional theism affirms), then we should not wonder that each of us has intrinsic dignity and worth, that we are morally responsible agents, that we have the capacity to recognize moral truths, and that we have certain moral obligations. It should, further, be noted that morality relates only to *persons*—not to rocks or nonpersonal entities like ants, rats or chimps, which are not morally responsible and have no moral obligations.

But if God does not exist, then we can rightly ask: *"On what basis* should I think that I have intrinsic dignity and worth? If there are moral laws to the universe, then why think that they have to do only with us humans and not other living organisms?"

Of course, people can be atheists or nontheists (i.e., who do not believe in a personal God) and *still* share the same moral values as theists (who believe in a personal God). Furthermore, they can develop moral systems which assert the same kinds of values that the theist affirms. This is not surprising since atheists too have been made in the image of a good God—even though they do not acknowledge this. So the issue to face is not, "Do I *recognize* certain moral values to be objectively true?" Rather, it is, "If I recognize these moral values to be true, which viewpoint offers the *best foundation* for these moral values?"

6. "If God existed, we would certainly *expect* objective moral values to exist." Explain.

7. If there were no God, how would your way of thinking about what is good and right be affected?

8. Look again at verses 35-36. According to Jesus, why should we love our enemies?

9. Read verses 32-36. Contrast Jesus' words to both utilitarianism and naturalism.

10. What *motivates* you to do the right thing when there is no obvious benefit or even opposition?

11. Consider a situation or difficult choice you wish you could revisit. How has your thinking changed given what you've discovered in this study? How would you now respond differently?

■ GOING FURTHER

A striking contrast to Jesus' teaching in Luke 6 is found in Judges 18. Its writer ominously observes, "In those days Israel had no king; everyone did as he saw fit" (Judges 17:6; 21:25). Consider how different the situation might have been if the people in Judges 18 had recognized the inherent worth of their neighbors and the reality of God's call upon their lives.

Additional Reading

For an extensive discussion of this question see John Hare, *Why Bother Being Good? The Place of God in the Moral Life* (Downers Grove, Ill.: InterVarsity Press, 2002).

PSALM 25:1-14

I t's perfectly fine to maintain that truth and falsity exist, that an objective reality exists, that moral right and wrong exist, and that some kind of exclusivism in religion exists. And the reason that this is perfectly fine is that *objective truth is unavoidable.* After all, if we attempt to reject it, we'll do so on the basis of reasons we take to be true and not false.

But if objective truth, reality and morality exist, then this has certain implications for me. It means living in accordance with these truths rather than pretending they don't exist.

■ OPEN

Name some people who have inspired you to greatness. What about them inspires you? Do you find yourself different in their presence? How?

■ STUDY

"The Psalms are a mirror of our souls," notes Bible scholar Tremper Longman. Psalm 25 is a heartfelt prayer of trust and request for God's guidance and deliverance in the face of enemies. The psalmist David declares that God is good and worthy of his hope and worship. He confidently asserts to God, "No one whose hope is in you will ever be put to shame." This psalm is an acrostic poem; each verse begins with the successive letters of the Hebrew alphabet. **Read Psalm 25:1-14.**

¹*To you, O LORD, I lift up my soul;*
² *in you I trust, O my God.*
  Do not let me be put to shame,
    nor let my enemies triumph over me.
³*No one whose hope is in you*
    will ever be put to shame,
  but they will be put to shame
    who are treacherous without excuse.
⁴*Show me your ways, O LORD,*
    teach me your paths;
⁵*guide me in your truth and teach me,*
    for you are God my Savior,
    and my hope is in you all day long.
⁶*Remember, O LORD, your great mercy and love,*
    for they are from of old.
⁷*Remember not the sins of my youth*
    and my rebellious ways;
  according to your love remember me,
    for you are good, O LORD.
⁸*Good and upright is the LORD;*
    therefore he instructs sinners in his ways.
⁹*He guides the humble in what is right*
    and teaches them his way.
¹⁰*All the ways of the LORD are loving and faithful*
    for those who keep the demands of his covenant.
¹¹*For the sake of your name, O LORD,*

forgive my iniquity, though it is great.
¹²*Who, then, is the man that fears the LORD?*
　　He will instruct him in the way chosen for him.
¹³*He will spend his days in prosperity,*
　　and his descendants will inherit the land.
¹⁴*The LORD confides in those who fear him;*
　　he makes his covenant known to them.

1. Look at verses 1-3. What is David's view of God? What is the relationship between verse 3 and verses 1 and 2?

2. What does the psalmist ask for in verses 4 and 5, and what are his expectations?

3. How is God described in verses 6-10?

4. If you were to write your own list, how would you describe God? Why?

What difference does God's existence make regarding the inherent worth of humans? The naturalist and the theist offer conflicting views on the nature of persons. If the God of theism exists, then personhood is not an accidental, derivative, late-arriving feature of the universe. Rather, the physical universe itself is the result of the creative act of a supreme Personal Being, who has also created us in his image. In this regard at least, persons play a central role in the grand scheme of things. If the source of all value is himself personal, then we have reason for believing that "persons have inherent value" is necessarily and eternally true—it was true before human persons ever graced this planet. Further, the moral point of view itself reflects the very nature of God and is therefore transcendent and objective rather than merely subjective and an instrument of survival. For at least these considerations, God's existence does indeed have a bearing upon the question of human dignity.

5. Why should we have reason for believing that "persons have inherent value"?

6. Look above at verse 14. How does this promise underscore that you have inherent value to God?

God has the *moral authority* to demand our unqualified obedience only if morality applies to God. Immanuel Kant observes that if we cannot meaningfully ascribe moral qualities to God, then "the concept of God's will still remaining to us—one drawn from such characteristics as lust for glory and domination and bound up with frightful ideas of power and vengefulness—would inevitably be the basis for a moral system which would be in direct opposition to morality."

Such a system of ethics would be "opposed" to morality because one's only motivation for obeying God would be of a nonmoral nature: God is very powerful and can become very angry when we refuse to obey. Christian morality that is not rooted in a sound understanding of God's *moral* right to command reduces to a system of hypothetical imperatives: *If you wish not to suffer everlasting punishment, then you had best do what he says!* C. S. Lewis does not pull punches here. He suggests that if our obedience to God is devoid of meaningful moral content then "we should be equally ready to obey an omnipotent fiend." In short, unless we may meaningfully assert that God is good, God's moral authority is reduced to sheer power and our motives for worshiping and obeying him are strictly out of self-regard rather than from a sense of duty. The answer to the question "Why ought one to be moral?" echoes that of the egoist: *because it serves your own interests in the long run.*

7. "God has the *moral authority* to demand our unqualified obedience only if morality applies to God." What's the difference between obeying God out of a sense of moral responsibility to his goodness, on the one hand, and obeying God out of a sensible fear of his power?

Which motivation inspires you more? Why?

8. What is the psalmist's motivation for obeying God? Does he see God as an "omnipotent fiend" or omnipotent friend? See especially verses 8-14.

God is necessarily holy, loving, kind, just, and so on, and these attributes of God comprise the Good. God's moral character expresses itself toward us in the form of certain commandments, which become for us our moral duties. Hence, God's commandments are not arbitrary, but necessarily flow from his own nature. They are necessary expressions of the way God is.

The atheist might press, "But why think that God's nature constitutes the Good?" Now in one sense, the answer to that question is that there just isn't anything else available. There has to be some explanatory ultimate, some stopping point, and we've seen that without God there are no objective moral values. Therefore, if there are objective moral values, they cannot be based in anything but God! In addition, however, God's nature is an appropriate stopping point for the standard of goodness. For by definition, God is a being who is worthy of worship. When you think about what it means to worship someone, then it is evident that only a being which is the embodiment of all moral goodness is worthy to be worshiped.[3]

[3]William Lane Craig, *God, Are You There?* (Norcross, Ga.: RZIM, 1999), pp. 39-40.

9. What reasons do we have for believing God is the appropriate stopping point for the standard of goodness?

10. What do think it means to worship someone?

11. Return to your answers to question 3. Would you *want* to worship such a God? Why or why not?

■ GOING FURTHER

Write out your thoughts about the idea that God is good and that he "confides in those who fear him." Spend some time also reading through Psalm 145—another psalm of David—and even praying that God would reveal his goodness and love toward you.

Additional Reading

For a brief but helpful discussion on the goodness of God, see chapter 16, "Goodness and Severity," in J. I. Packer's classic book *Knowing God* (Downers Grove, Ill.: InterVarsity Press, 1993).

Leader's Notes

Leading a small group discussion can be an enjoyable and rewarding experience. But it can also be *scary*—especially if you've never done it before. If this is your feeling, you're in good company. When God asked Moses to lead the Israelites out of Egypt, he replied, "O LORD, please send someone else to do it" (Ex 4:13). It was the same with Solomon, Jeremiah and Timothy, but God helped these people in spite of their weaknesses, and he will help you as well.

You don't need to be an expert on the Bible or a trained teacher to lead a group discussion. The idea behind these studies is that the leader guides group members in their exploration of critical questions in the life of faith. This method of learning will allow group members to remember much more of what is said than a lecture would.

These studies are designed to be led easily. As a matter of fact, the flow of questions is so natural that you may feel that the studies lead themselves. This study guide is also flexible. You can use it with a variety of groups—student, professional, neighborhood or church groups. Each study takes around sixty minutes in a group setting.

There are some important facts to know about group dynamics

and encouraging discussion. The suggestions listed below should enable you to effectively and enjoyably fulfill your role as leader.

■ PREPARING FOR THE STUDY

1. Ask God to help you understand and apply the material in each session for your own life. Unless this happens, you will not be prepared to lead others. Pray too for the various members of the group. Ask God to open your hearts to the message of his Word and motivate you to action.

2. Read the introduction to the entire guide to get an overview of the entire book and the issues which will be explored.

3. As you begin each study, read and reread the assigned material to familiarize yourself with it.

4. Carefully work through each question in the study. Spend time in meditation and reflection as you consider how to respond.

5. Write your thoughts and responses in the space provided in the study guide. This will help you to express your understanding of the material clearly.

6. It might help to have a Bible dictionary handy. Use it to look up any unfamiliar words, names or places. (For additional help on how to study a passage, see chapter five of *How to Lead a LifeGuide Bible Study,* InterVarsity Press.)

7. Consider how the Scripture applies to your life. Remember that the group will follow your lead in responding to the studies. They will not go any deeper than you do.

8. Once you have finished your own study of the passage, familiarize yourself with the leader's notes for the study you are leading. These are designed to help you in several ways. First, they tell

you the purpose the study guide author had in mind when writing the study. Take time to think through how the study questions work together to accomplish that purpose. Second, the notes provide you with additional background information for various questions. This information can be useful when people have difficulty understanding or answering a question. Third, the leader's notes can alert you to potential problems you may encounter during the study.

9. If you wish to remind yourself of anything mentioned in the leader's notes, make a note to yourself below that question in the study.

■ LEADING THE STUDY

1. Begin the study on time. Open with prayer, asking God to help the group to understand and apply the material being discussed.

2. Be sure that everyone in your group has a study guide. Encourage the group to prepare beforehand for each discussion by reading the introduction to the guide and by working through the questions in that week's session.

3. At the beginning of your first time together, explain that these studies are meant to be discussions, not lectures. Encourage the members of the group to participate. However, do not put pressure on those who may be hesitant to speak during the first few sessions. You may want to suggest the following guidelines to your group.

• Stick to the topic being discussed.

• Your responses should be based on the material provided and not on outside authorities such as commentaries or speakers.

- Only rarely should you refer to other portions of the Bible. This allows for everyone to participate in in-depth study on equal ground.

- Anything said in the group is considered confidential and will not be discussed outside the group unless specific permission is given to do so.

- We will listen attentively to each other and provide time for each person present to talk.

- We will pray for each other.

4. Have a group member read the introduction at the beginning of the discussion.

5. Every session begins with a group discussion question. The question or activity is meant to be used before the passage is read. The question introduces the theme of the study and encourages group members to begin to open up. Encourage as many members as possible to participate, and be ready to get the discussion going with your own response.

This section is designed to reveal where our thoughts or feelings need to be transformed by the renewing of our minds. That is why it is especially important not to read the passage to the group members before the discussion question is asked. The passage will tend to color the honest reactions people would otherwise give because they are, of course, supposed to think the way the Bible does.

You may want to supplement the group discussion question with an icebreaker to help people to get comfortable. See the community section of *Small Group Idea Book* for more ideas.

6. Have a group member (or members if the passage is long) read aloud the textual material as it occurs in the session. Then give people several minutes to read the passage again silently so that they can take it all in.

7. As you ask the questions, keep in mind that they are designed to be used just as they are written. You may simply read them aloud. Or you may prefer to express them in your own words. There may be times when it is appropriate to deviate from the study guide. For example, a question may have already been answered. If so, move on to the next question. Or someone may raise an important question not covered in the guide. Take time to discuss it, but try to keep the group from going off on tangents.

8. Avoid answering your own questions. If necessary, repeat or re-phrase them until they are clearly understood. Or point out something you read in the leader's notes to clarify the context or meaning. An eager group quickly becomes passive and silent if they think the leader will do most of the talking.

9. Don't be afraid of silence. People may need time to think about the question before formulating their answers.

10. Don't be content with just one answer. Ask, "What do the rest of you think?" or "Anything else?" until several people have given answers to the question.

11. Acknowledge all contributions. Try to be affirming whenever possible. Never reject an answer. If it is clearly off-base, ask, "Which verse led you to that conclusion?" or again, "What do the rest of you think?"

12. Don't expect every answer to be addressed to you, even though this will probably happen at first. As group members become

more at ease, they will begin to truly interact with each other. This is one sign of healthy discussion.

13. Don't be afraid of controversy. It can be very stimulating. If you don't resolve an issue completely, don't be frustrated. Move on and keep it in mind for later. A subsequent study may solve the problem.

14. Periodically summarize what the group has said to that point. This helps to draw together the various ideas mentioned and gives continuity to the discussion. But don't preach.

15. Give an opportunity during the session for people to talk about what they are learning.

16. Conclude your time together with conversational prayer. Ask for God's help in working through the implications of the discussion.

17. End on time.

■ COMPONENTS OF SMALL GROUPS

A healthy small group should do more than study the Bible. There are four components to consider as you structure your time together.

- *Nurture.* Small groups help us to grow in our knowledge and love of God. Bible study is the key to making this happen and is the foundation of your small group.

- *Community.* Small groups are a great place to develop deep friendships with other Christians. Allow time for informal interaction before and after each discussion. Plan activities and games that will help you get to know each other. Spend time having fun together—going on a picnic or cooking dinner together.

- *Worship and prayer.* Your study will be enhanced by spending time praising God together in prayer or song. Pray for each other's needs—and keep track of how God is answering prayer in your group. Ask God to help you to apply what you are learning in your study.

• *Outreach.* Reaching out to others can be a practical way of applying what you are learning, and it will keep your group from becoming self-focused. Host a series of evangelistic discussions for your friends or neighbors. Clean up the yard of an elderly friend. Serve at a soup kitchen together, or spend a day working on a Habitat house.

Many more suggestions and helps in each of these areas are found in *Small Group Idea Book.* Information on building a small group can be found in *Small Group Leaders' Handbook* and *The Big Book on Small Groups* (both from InterVarsity Press). Reading through one of these books would be worth your time.

STUDY 1

Does Relativism Work?

JOSHUA 24:14-28

Purpose: **To show that though relativism may be popular, it contradicts its own claims.**

QUESTION 1. The verb *serve* appears thirteen times in ten verses and connotes something other than perfunctory duty. The word used throughout the Old Testament is also translated as "worship" and "honor." When used of God, it is a call to entrust our whole selves to him in reverence and loyalty. For example, the imperative found in verse 14 is the same one used in Psalm 100:2 and should be understood in the same context: "*Worship* the LORD with gladness; come before him with joyful song." (This is from the NIV; the KJV and NASB render the word as "serve.") The call to "serve" or "choose" God is typical covenant language. God promises to be the sovereign protector, and the recipients of the covenant in turn declare their allegiance and service to him. Given that other nations held to polytheism (the belief in many gods), the LORD God sets an explicit choice before his people: You must choose whom you will serve.

It is important to examine this passage within the context of chapter 24. As in other covenant renewal ceremonies, the stipulations in verses 14-26 are first preceded by a reminder of God's faithfulness and acts of lovingkindness toward his people (see 24:1-13). The NIV begins verse 14 with "And now," yet the ESV and NASB provide a clearer understanding with the implied "Now *therefore*." Bible scholars refer to this as an *indicative-imperative*, meaning that the declarative statement calls forth an imperative action or command. That is, God's past actions reveal him to be true and faithful; *therefore* our response should be to devote our allegiance and trust to him.

QUESTION 2. God presents this choice through Joshua: "But if serving the LORD seems undesirable to you, then choose for yourselves this day whom you will serve." "Undesirable" literally reads "evil (or bad) in your eyes." By using such provocative language God communicates that he recognizes the appeal of the gods of Canaan that offered instant release from hardship and caused his people to question his provision and goodness. Again, God rehearses the fulfillments of his promises to his people through Abraham, Jacob, Moses and Joshua earlier in this chapter to remind his people that he alone has been their deliverance and salvation.

QUESTION 3. Like God's provocative declaration in verse 15, Joshua responds with a challenge to the people's ready and perhaps unreflective answer that they will serve God. Jesus offers a similar response to Peter before and after he denies him, causing Peter to consider the life-altering commitment he has made (see Jn 13:37-38 and Jn 20:15-19).

QUESTIONS 5-6. Relativists certainly give the impression that they believe their view is true for everyone. And not only that, they often try to *persuade* others to believe their perspective. In fact, they are often willing to give *objective* reasons—that is, reasons that are true, independent of anyone's viewpoint—for why relativism is true and absolutism is false. For example, relativists might say, "So many people believe different things; therefore relativism is the inescapable conclusion." But we can point out that *at the very least* (a) their *basis* for holding to relativism (i.e., that so many people disagree) is *true*—*not false*, and that (b) the relativist's conclusion about the inevitability of relativism is also true, not false. So in actuality, the relativist is an absolutist in relativist's clothing.

Furthermore, we could take *any* relativistic statement and turn it into an objective truth-claim. All we have to do is add, before each slogan: *"It is true that"* or *"It is objectively true for everyone that . . . everything is relative"* or *"It's true that this is your or my reality"* or *"It is undeniably true that that's true for you but not for me."* You get the idea!

QUESTIONS 7-10. Ravi Zacharias elaborates, "One surprising illusion under which the modern critic of Christianity lives is the belief that Christianity is the only system of belief that is exclusivistic. This assumption reveals a significant ignorance of all of the major world-views present today. In reality, every system is implicitly exclusivistic. Buddhism was born out of a repudiation of two cardinal doctrines of Hinduism. Gautama Buddha rejected the Vedas as the ultimate truth and denounced the caste system outrightly. The caste system, of course, was inextricably woven into the doctrine of reincarnation and hence, the nuance of difference in Buddhism's doctrine of transmigration.

"Sikhism in effect rejected both Hinduism and Buddhism. And in a valiant attempt to pull everything together, Baha'aism, an attempt at religious universalism, deveined all of them and excluded the exclusivists. Even a cursory understanding of Islam conveys its radical exclusivism. Islam is not only exclusive theologically, it is also exclusive linguistically. According to Islamic teaching, the sole, sufficient, and consummate miracle in Islam is the Koran, which is only recognizable in the Arabic. Any translation diminshes the primary source and desacralizes the verbiage. And I might add, that it is not merely an understanding of Arabic that is required, but a sophisticated knowledge of it. As for antitheism, it rejects all theistic viewpoints and treats their beliefs as orphaned from reason. So let us be honest; let's remove this scar attributed by antitheists to Christianity that supposedly mars the otherwise beautiful countenance of religious or secular tolerance.

"The issue then is not whether the belief system you espouse— monotheistic, atheistic, pantheistic, or otherwise—is exclusive. The issue is whether the answers to the four basic questions of life pertaining to origin, meaning, morality, and destiny within the context of each of these world-views meet the tests of truth" (*Can Man Live Without God?* [Dallas: Word, 1994], pp. 125-26).

STUDY 2

Is Sincerity Enough?

ACTS 26:1-29

Purpose: **To show that the idea that truth is objective is inescapable and that sincerity is not enough.**

QUESTIONS 2-4. Bible scholar I. Howard Marshall observes that

Paul gives an autobiographical defense "so as to stress that he was a fervent adherent to the Jewish faith and to pave the way for the claim that the Christian faith is continuous with Judaism. Then Paul describes his initial hostility to the church. This point may be intended to indicate that he did not embrace Christianity blindly; it must have been an overwhelming conviction which led to his change of attitude. . . .

"The word *hope* is a key term in Paul's defence (23:6; 24:15; 26:6f.; 28:20). It refers to the believing expectation that God will fulfil the promises and prophecies in the Old Testament, and for Paul it refers specifically to the belief that these promises have been and will be fulfilled in Jesus. The question at issue is thus whether the Jews believe in God's promises. . . .

"[A]t issue was Paul's belief in the resurrection. He takes the offensive by asking why it should be thought incredible that *God raises the dead.* . . . For Pharisees there should have been no difficulty, since in general they did believe in the resurrection. The Sadducees did not believe in it, but they could well be asked why they regarded it as something God could not accomplish. But of course, although Paul asks the question in general terms, the real point at issue is the resurrection of Jesus which attested that he was the Messiah: why should that be thought incredible?" (I. Howard Marshall, *Acts,* The Tyndale New Testament Commentaries [Downers Grove, Ill.: InterVarsity Press, 1980], pp. 390-92).

QUESTIONS 5-6. It might be beneficial to note other slogans that fit into this category. Let's try this one: *"There are no facts—only interpretations."* This is commonly asserted, but does asserting this statement itself make an *exception* to this statement? Clearly, the person who says that there are no facts—only interpretations—believes that this statement is *factual*, not merely *interpretive!*

Here's another: *"There is no reality—only appearances."* (As Woody Allen once mused: "What if everything is an illusion and nothing exists? In that case I definitely overpaid for my carpet.") The person who declares this believes that *at least this statement properly reflects reality!* And, furthermore, if there is no reality, aren't the *appearances themselves* real?

A final slogan to note is this one: *"Question authority!"* Although there is undoubtedly a tendency for, say, political authorities to overstep their bounds, there is something fundamentally flawed in the assumption of this quip. This slogan *presupposes an authority of its own*, doesn't it? It essentially says this: "Question all authority, but don't question my authority!" Some kind of objective (or, dare we say, *authoritative*) standpoint will be inevitable; objectivity is inescapable. Those who deny it will make themselves exceptions to their own rule.

Again, those who reduce all that we think and do to genetics, environment, reproduction and survival, or language do one of two things: (a) they *contradict themselves* by acting as though they have escaped the influences everyone else is subject to (the self-excepting fallacy); or (b) they *say nothing at all* since what they express is nothing more than the product of those influences.

QUESTION 8. The expression "to kick against the goads" is found in classical Greek and other Jewish writings as well. The Greek writer Euripides advised one person, "You are mortal, he [Dionysus] is a god. If I were you I would control my rage and sacrifice to him, rather than kick against the pricks." The proverb attested to the unchangeable nature of objective reality—as humans, we are not wholly able to change or determine our past, present and future—and to the conscience's inability to resolve this struggle. Some commentators suggest Paul struggled with recurrent feelings of guilt over Stephen's stoning. (See Marshall, *Acts,* p. 395.)

STUDY 3
Are Judgments Inevitable?
1 CORINTHIANS 5

Purpose: To show that each of us has limits regarding tolerance and that judgments are inevitable.

QUESTIONS 1-2. Regarding verses 1 and 2, New Testament scholar Leon Morris writes, "That it *does not occur even among pagans* does not mean that it never occurred, but that it was infrequent and that it was condemned as evil. It was, for example, forbidden by Roman law, and, of course, by the Old Testament (Lv. 18:8; 20:11; Dt. 22:30; 27:20). . . .

"The attitude of the church members to this happening had been all wrong. They were *proud* ('puffed up'; see . . . [1 Corinthians 4:6]); their view of their superior standing, rather than a decent Christian humility, had governed their behaviour. Evidently they saw their Christian freedom as giving them licence for almost any kind of conduct (*cf.* 6:12; 10:23)" (Leon Morris, *1 Corinthians,* The Tyndale New Testament Commentaries [Downers Grove, Ill.: InterVarsity Press, 1999], p. 83).

QUESTION 3. Paul's exhortation to "hand over to Satan" the offender is found elsewhere only in 1 Timothy 1:20, where he excommunicates two members for teaching blasphemy. Paul makes a sharp distinction between the church, Christ's body, and the world, which is under the rule of Satan. Yet he also expresses the hope of such judgment: that the offender's "spirit [be] saved on the day of the

Lord" (v. 5). Though Paul's words are harsh, his intent is similar to that of the father in the story of the prodigal son in John 15:11-32. The father (who represents God) allows the younger son to take his inheritance and leave home, knowing that his years away will reveal the futility of living apart from him. Indeed, after the son "squandered his wealth in wild living" and suffered through a famine, he "came to his senses" and returned home, admitting to himself, "Father, I have sinned against heaven and against you" (see vv. 13-18). Before he even reaches home, his father runs to welcome him. Sadly, of course, not all who go astray return with remorse and desire for fellowship—or perhaps worse, they return only to be met by condemnation and unforgiveness. However, Scripture affirms that repentance and restoration is the goal of discipline. Leon Morris comments, "Paul sees the punishment as remedial: though the flesh be destroyed it is so that *his spirit* may be *saved*. That this means saved in the fullest sense is made clear by the addition, *on the day of the Lord.* At the final day of judgment he expects to see the disciplined offender among the Lord's people" (Morris, *1 Corinthians*, p. 86).

QUESTION 5. Ravi Zacharias cautions, "If the human spirit is to survive and every legitimate discipline to find fruitful expression, truth cannot be sacrificed at the altar of a pretended tolerance. All religions, plainly and simply, cannot be true. Some beliefs are false, and we know them to be false. So it does no good to put a halo on the notion of tolerance as if everything could be equally true. To deem all beliefs equally true is sheer nonsense for the simple reason that to deny that statement would also, then, be true. But if the denial of the statement is also true, then all religions are not true" (Ravi Zacharias, *Jesus Among Other Gods* [Nashville: Word, 2000], p. 4).

QUESTIONS 6-7. Just as a little yeast changes the consistency of dough, so sin alters us. *Yeast* in Scripture is often a metaphor for evil and was prohibited during Passover as a reminder that God delivered the Israelites from Egypt. Leon Morris observes, "So Paul speaks of *a new batch without yeast.* The Christian church is not just the old society patched up. It is radically new (2 Corinthians 5:17). . . . *For* introduces the reason for this confident assertion. The great fact that makes all things new is that *Christ, our Passover, has been sacrificed.* . . . Paul is using this imagery to remind his readers that the death of Christ had delivered them from slavery to evil and made them the people of God. There is emphasis on emergence to new life, and here the symbolism of yeast makes an important point. Ancient Israel was commanded to remove all yeast before the sacrifice (Exodus 12:15; 13:7), and in Paul's day a feature of Passover observance was a solemn search for and destruction of all yeast before the feast began. This had to be done before the *pasha*, the kid or lamb, was offered in the temple. Paul points out that *Christ, our Passover* has already been sacrificed. It is time and more than time that all yeast (*i.e.* evil) was put away" (Morris, *1 Corinthians,* pp. 87-88).

QUESTION 7. Social scientists label the attempt to hold to two opposing views as "cognitive dissonance." The late Christian apologist Greg Bahnsen surmised, "There is something of a cognitive mess at the core of our lives. We are inconsistent in our choices, incoherent in our convictions, persuaded where we ought not to be, and deluded that we know ourselves transparently" (Greg Bahnsen, "The Crucial Concept of Self-Deception in Presuppositional Apologetics" in *Westminster Theological Journal* 57 [1995], pp. 1-31; available online at www.cmfnow.com/articles/pa207.htm).

Ravi Zacharias illustrates this dilemma in an individual he encountered while discussing sociologist Daniel Bell's definition of culture: "'the effort to provide a coherent set of answers to the existential questions that confront all human beings in the passage of their lives.' . . . A student stormed up to the microphone and bellowed, 'Who told you culture is a search for coherence? Where do you get that idea from? This idea of coherence is a Western idea.'

"Rather surprised, I replied by reminding her that all I had done was to present a sociologist's definition. 'Ah! Words! Just words!' she shouted back.

" 'Let me ask you this then,' I pleaded with her. 'Do you want my answer to be coherent?' At that moment, laughter rippled through the auditorium. She herself was stymied for a few moments. 'But that's language, isn't it?' she retorted.

"So I asked her if language had anything to do with reality. 'Don't words refer to something?' I asked her. 'If you are seeking an intelligible answer from me, mustn't there be correspondence between my words and reality?' " (Ravi Zacharias, "The Postmodern Predicament: Absence of Coherence," *A Slice of Infinity*, online at www.rzim.org/publications/slicetran.php?sliceid=6).

STUDY 4

Can We Have Moral Values Without God?

ROMANS 1:16-20, 28-32; 2:1-4

Purpose: **To show that no one consistently holds to moral relativism because it is plainly unlivable.**

QUESTION 1. Paul associates *power, righteousness* and *faith* with the gospel: God's plan of salvation through the life, death and resurrection of Jesus Christ. Through the gift of faith in Christ (Eph 2:8-9) we are put "in the right" before God and are empowered to love and serve him and others.

QUESTION 2. We suppress the truth of God and his moral law whether through willful denial, misdirected affections or unexamined belief. Suppressing the truth, the skeptic attempts to resist God, though "his eternal power and divine nature have been clearly perceived every since the foundation of the world" (Rom 1:20), and the believer finds rationale to give in to sin. As Paul writes a few verses later, "They exchanged the truth of God for a lie, and worshiped and served created things rather than the Creator" (v. 25).

Greg Bahnsen astutely observes, "That self-deception which is practiced by all unregenerate men according to the Apostle Paul's incisive description in Romans 1:18ff. is at once religiously momentous and yet philosophically enigmatic. . . . We must say in conformity to Romans 1 that in some sense the non-Christian knows and does not know God. In some sense, he believes, but disbelieves in God. In some sense, he is unconscious of suppressing the truth and still responsibly conscious of doing so. So then, what might prove especially beneficial would be for us to give some sense to these apparent paradoxes. . . .

"I would maintain, then, that self-deception, as a form of deception, involves believing false propositions. Further, the mistaken believing which is involved is fully genuine believing. We do not here speak of 'belief' in some odd, defective, or 'twilight' sense. The self-deceiver is not merely feigning ignorance or being an obvious hypocrite. He is concerned with the truth and makes efforts, albeit strained, to sustain his false belief as rational. . . . He must say that he really believes the false proposition, or else he would not be 'deceived' after all. This is not simply half-belief or near-belief, for that proposal would reduce self-deception to mere vacillation, lack of confidence, or insincerity. There is no lack of evidence for the self-deceiver's full-fledged believing; it is just that we have too many beliefs of his for which there is adequate evidence—beliefs which are incompatible" (Bahnsen, "The Crucial Concept of Self-Deception in Presuppositional Apologetics").

QUESTIONS 7-8. Ravi Zacharias relates a particularly illuminating sequence of news reports: "The newscast's first story was a survey. The first question posed to the people asked if words meant anything at all. Words such as 'affair' and 'adultery'—do they have particular meanings or could the person speaking fuse them with his or her own meaning? In our truth-by-survey culture, if you will, the journalists asked people if anything meant anything anymore.

"Having concluded that there were significant variances in the way people used words, the journalists next inquired if morality was purely a personal matter, or were there indeed absolutes? Every person on the street interviewed answered the same way. 'No,' they said, 'There is no objective morality, we have to define it on our own terms.'

"So, the first item was whether or not words were subject to the user. The second was whether or not morality was a thoroughly personal matter.

"Then, having settled on an answer which left the individual sovereign over reality, the third news item was a warning to a tyrannical world leader. If he did not stop playing his word games, we were going to start bombing his country. . . . How ironic, I thought.

"We claim moral autonomy for ourselves and deny the correspondence of words to reality, except when we deal with others who play the same game. In short, our relativism is unlivable" (Zacharias, "The

Postmodern Predicament: Relativism Is Unlivable").

QUESTION 9. Jesus states in Matthew 7:1-2, "Do not judge, or you too will be judged. For in the same way you judge others, you will be judged, and with the measure you use, it will be measured to you." He is not saying that we are not to exercise judgment, but rather that we are to pay careful attention to the "plank in [our] own eye" (v. 4). Jesus confirms there is a moral law that we intuitively understand whether we submit to it or judge others by it.

STUDY 5

Why Should We Be Good?

LUKE 6:27-36

Purpose: **To show that a morality which respects the inherent worth and dignity of human beings cannot be consistently sustained apart from the existence of God.**

QUESTION 2. According to Jesus, to love one's enemies is to "do good to those who hate you, bless those who curse you, [and] pray for those who mistreat you." Notice that Jesus' view of love is more than romantic sentiment or emotion. It is *agapē,* the way *God* loves, "love even of the unlovely, love which is not drawn out by merit in the beloved but which proceeds from the fact that the lover chooses to be a loving person" (Leon Morris, *Luke,* Tyndale New Testament Commentaries [Downers Grove, Ill.: InterVarsity Press, 1994], p. 142).

Another understanding of such love is the Hebrew word *hesed,* or "loving-kindness." The word is so rich in meaning that scholars say it is not translatable in English. *Hesed* is used throughout the Old Testament in reference to God's covenantal relationship with his people.

It denotes God's favor and faithfulness, the wideness of his love and mercy, as well as his chastening.

Jesus' four statements reveal that *agapē* love is best understood as a *verb*. Likewise, commentator Daniel Block remarks, *hesed* is "that quality that moves a person to act for the benefit of another without respect to the advantage that it might bring to the one who expresses it. . . . [T]his quality is expressed fundamentally in action rather than word or emotion" (Daniel Block, *Judges, Ruth*, vol. 6, New American Commentary [Nashville: Broadman & Holman, 1999], pp. 605-6).

QUESTION 3. Darrell Bock wisely observes, "Jesus decries our culture's version of love. What is required to possess true love is an understanding of what it is to be loved by God and how God wishes one to love. At the center of Jesus' sermon is a unique concept of love. This love cannot be reduced merely to the 'golden rule'; it is love that is golden even when everything around us is not.

"Jesus does not wait to make his point on the unusual character of such love. . . . Jesus' call is specific: *love your enemies, do good to those who hate you, bless those who curse you, pray for those who mistreat you.* Whether in attitude, action, word or intercession, the enemy is to be loved. . . .

"Jesus offers what became known in the sixteenth century as the 'golden rule': *Do to others as you would have them do to you.* The verse has Old Testament roots (Lev 19:18). . . . Jesus is not saying, 'Do good deeds for others so they will return the favor.' Instead he is calling for actions of love regardless of how the other responds" (Darrell Bock, *Luke*, The IVP New Testament Commentary Series [Downers Grove, Ill.: InterVarsity Press, 1994], pp. 122-23, 125).

QUESTIONS 4-5. The common response of utilitarians in determining what they wish to do is "it depends." Does utilitarianism imply that bullfighting is wrong? The answer is: *it depends*. It depends on just *how much* happiness or pleasure is produced by the sport, weighed out against just how much suffering the animal endures. It is not difficult to see how utilitarian calculations could yield the conclusion that the suffering of one animal is a relatively small price to pay for the euphoria of thousands of bullfighting enthusiasts.

Here we encounter a serious and persistent objection to utilitarianism as an ethical theory: it seems to have iniquitous implications. I need not look beyond the pages of history to find an example in which the arena is filled not with bullfighting enthusiasts, but with people who are there for Family Fun Night to witness human tragedy firsthand. It's the Christians versus the Lions, and the Christians have a worse win-loss record than the New York Mets. Isn't it wrong to throw our neighbors to wild beasts for entertainment purposes? One would have thought so. Again, the utilitarian's answer must be: *it depends*. It depends on just how intense the human suffering is and how heavily this suffering weighs in against the pleasure to be had by the spectators.

The general problem is that there appears to be no necessary connection between an action's being the one that produces the greatest net utility and its being fair or just to each member of the moral community. Of course, the utilitarian may object that there is a built-in concern for justice or fairness. But equal consideration and justice are two very different things, given a utilitarian approach. The fact that my potential agony is fully and fairly factored in as the utilitarians do their calculation does not necessarily preserve me from being forced to do the half-time show in the arena. For it may well be the case that the best way to achieve long-term happiness for the community is precisely that course of action that I fear the most.

QUESTION 7. Regarding how naturalism and theism differ in their views of human beings, if Darwin's account of the origin and nature of human morality is correct, then it is difficult to see how one could expect the "moral law within" to be the ground of human dignity or inherent value. On the Darwinian scheme, morality is a "device of survival in social organisms."

Our common moral experience seems to presuppose a certain kind of moral principle—namely, respect for persons—but the naturalist is unable to accommodate such a principle within his worldview. Have we any good reason for supposing that theism fares better than naturalism? For example, I have implied that the very notion of human dignity makes sense only if God exists. What difference does God's existence make regarding the inherent worth of humans?

The Darwinian account of human origins implies that all uniquely human characteristics, such as rationality and moral agency, are themselves of mere *instrumental* value as nature has "selected" these as means to human survival. Even if the naturalist were not committed to wholesale subjectivism, he would be hard-pressed to specify why anyone should suppose that humans have any special worth or dignity. Our first observation, then, is that *moral principles such as respect for persons are not indifferent to one's choice of worldview.*

QUESTIONS 8-9. Jesus grounds the reason we should love our enemies in his conclusion: "because [God] is kind to the ungrateful and wicked." He adds, "Be merciful, just as your Father is merciful." Our love is evidence that we are our Father's children, "sons of the Most High." Yes, God promises to reward those who love, but the focus of such reward is *relationship with him* and the blessings that flow from this relationship.

In stark contrast to the utilitarian, Jesus proclaims that we are to love the individual even when we have nothing to gain because he is made in God's image. And to the naturalist, Jesus suggests, such love is possible only because it proceeds from a heavenly Father: "We love because he first loved us" (1 Jn 4:10; cf. 4:7-8).

STUDY 6

Who Is the Lord?
PSALM 25:1-14

Purpose: **To show objective morals values can only be rooted in a good and just God.**

QUESTION 1. David views God as trustworthy and attentive to his prayer. As is common in the psalms, he voices a plea ("Do not let me be put to shame") and then answers it with an affirmation that God has spoken to him ("No one whose hope is in you will ever be put to shame"). Verse 3 is the assurance of God's response to his request in verses 1 and 2.

QUESTIONS 3-4. Among God's many attributes, David twice declares that God is "good" (vv. 7, 8). The goodness of God is a theme found throughout Scripture, for God's very essence is goodness. In Exodus 33:18-19, we read: "Then Moses said, 'Now show me your glory.' And the LORD said, 'I will cause my goodness to pass in front of you.'" Psalm 145:9 says, "The LORD is good to all; he has compassion on all he has made." For other references in the Psalms, see also 31:19; 34:8; 73:1; 86:5 ("good" is translated as "kind" in the NIV); 100:5 and 119:68. Moreover, Jesus declared, "No one is good—except God alone" (Mk 10:18; cf. Mt 19:17).

God is "good" neither in the trivial sense (that he is like himself)

nor in the sense that he fulfills obligations and duties that are im-
posed upon him from some independent moral standard. Rather,
God's goodness consists in the fact that he necessarily and perfectly
exemplifies the kind of character and conduct that we recognize as
morally good in our fellow human beings. God is good precisely because he is benevolent and just, merciful and forgiving, and these are
the very kinds of traits that we praise in ordinary moral discourse.
God is himself the source of our moral concepts. God is the Creator of the
very moral capacity that we employ when making moral judgments.
We recognize genuine virtues for what they are—whether in God or
fellow creatures—because we have been endowed with moral capac-
ities (included in what is called "the image of God"). In this way, the
moral light of human conscience is but a reflection of God's own nature, which is its source.

QUESTIONS 7, 9. God is the appropriate stopping point for the
standard of goodness because objective values necessarily flow from
him and by definition he is worthy of worship. Christian philosopher
William Lane Craig summarizes, "If God does not exist, then morality is just a human convention, that is to say, morality is wholly subjective and non-binding. We might act in precisely the same ways
that we do in fact act, but in the absence of God, such actions would
no longer count as good (or evil), since if God does not exist, objective moral values do not exist. Thus, we cannot truly be good without
God. On the other hand, if we do believe that moral values and duties
are objective, that provides moral grounds for believing in God. . . .

"In the Judeo-Christian tradition, the whole moral duty of man
can be summed up in the two great commandments: First, you shall
love the Lord your God with all your strength and with all your soul
and with all your heart and with all your mind, and, second, you

shall love your neighbor as yourself. On this foundation we can affirm the objective goodness and rightness of love, generosity, self-sacrifice, and equality, and condemn as objectively evil and wrong selfishness, hatred, abuse, discrimination, and oppression. . . .

"Despite the inequities of this life, in the end the scales of God's justice will be balanced. Thus, the moral choices we make in this life are infused with an eternal significance. We can with consistency make moral choices which run contrary to our self-interest and even undertake acts of extreme self-sacrifice, knowing that such decisions are not empty and ultimately meaningless gestures. Rather our moral lives have a paramount significance. So I think it is evident that theism provides a sound foundation for morality" (William Lane Craig, "The Indispensability of Theological Meta-Ethical Foundations for Morality" online article available at www.leaderu.com/offices/billcraig/docs/meta-eth.html).

QUESTION 8. David's *relationship* with God motivates him to obey him. The psalmist is a "man that fears the LORD" (v. 12). This fear is best described as *reverence* and *awe*. It is a recognition of God's omnipotence and splendor as well as his "great mercy and love" (v. 6). As David writes in the closing verse of the psalm before, "The LORD Almighty—he is the King of glory" (Ps 24:10). Such fear not only invokes worship but surrenders to trust, for "the LORD confides in those who fear him" (25:14). The Hebrew word for "confides" is translated as the "friendship of the LORD" and "secret of the LORD" in other Bible versions, denoting a trusting and open relationship. Indeed, Psalm 147:11 says, "The LORD delights in those who fear him, who put their hope in his unfailing love."